# ROCKSTAR / PAPERMAN / SCISSORHAND

Poems by Chigger Matthews

Kansas City  Spartan Press  Missouri

Spartan Press
Kansas City, Missouri
spartanpresskc.com

Copyright (c) Matthew Haines, 2018
First Edition 1 3 5 7 9 10 8 6 4 2
ISBN: 978-1-946642-49-3
LCCN: 2018940003

Design, edits and layout: Jason Ryberg
Cover image: Jon Lee Grafton
Author photo: Opalina Salas
All rights reserved. No part of this publication may be reproduced or transmitted in any form or by any means, electronic or mechanical, including photocopying, recording or by info retrieval system, without prior written permission from the author.

Spartan Press would like to thank Prospero's Books, The Fellowship of N-finite Jest, The Prospero Institute of Disquieted P/o/e/t/i/c/s, Will Leathem, Tom Wayne, Jeanette Powers, j. d. tulloch, Jon Bidwell, Jason Preu, Mark McClane, Tony Hayden and the whole Osage Arts Community.

This book is for my (chosen) family
without which I am not.

## CONTENTS

Opening Credits / 1

Eloquent / 3

Language / 4

Haben Sie Papieren? / 5

I Fall in Love / 7

Lily and I / 8

Pee-Shivers / 9

Truisms Form a Yes-Set / 11

*(paraphrasing Dale Carnegie)* / 12

Muses are People, People are Animals / 13

Road Smells / 14

I Say It out Loud / 15

She Said, Pt.1 / 16

She Said, Pt.2 / 17

Two Things: First, I Foolishly Write a Great Deal of My Work While Driving on the Long Stretches of Interstate Highway Between Readings (Sorry Maha) and Second, This Poem Is Called *Crash* / 18

Gee Thanks, Maha / 20

(for Steve Vogt) / 21

Hvarnuh! / 22

This Is the Test / 23

Four Lords and a Lady / 24

Ero / 25

Gasoline / 26

*Mani Padme Hum Shiva* / 27

I Know My Rights / 28

Introspect / 29

She-Wasps / 30

Firefly Royalty in Garden Regalia
  at Purple Dusk / 34

Ozark Knights / 36

(for Anna Pietrzak) / 39

Working on My Car / 40

Optimism and Confidence / 41

Memory / 42

And Anyway / 43

Sleep Walking / 45

A Mind Camp Intern Meditates with Dogs / 46

Four Seasons Poem / 47

Affluenza / 48

*Momento Mori* (from *The Travelers Guide
  to Psychometry*) / 49

Moonshot (from *The Travelers Guide
  to Psychometry*) / 51

Window Roller (from *The Travelers Guide
  to Psychometry*) / 53

Dirge of Lightning Bugs (from *The Travelers
  Guide to Psychometry*) / 55

LIGHTNING VAJRA! (from *The Travelers
  Guide to Psychometry*) / 57

The Universal Sign for Choking or *Ek-! Ek-!* / 59

*Hear me! For I am such and such a person.
Above all, do not mistake me for someone esle.*

-Friedrich Nietzsche

## Opening Credits

I
stepped
over
bleach
white
bone
picked
clean
by
buzzards,
pulverized
by
tires.

Noted
little
mashed
lunch
box
turtles
with
a
sigh.

Kept
walking
into
a
Southerly
wind
with
the
sun
on
my
shoulder
and
traffic
in
my
eyes.

# Eloquent

I've
often
wished
to
put

bird
calls

in
my
poetry.

Aren't
they
so
much
more
eloquent?

# Language

sometimes
the
water
looks
like
it's
flowing
backwards

which

is

weird

because

by

comparison

it
normally
is
something
that
cannot
be
expressed
by
language

## Haben Sie Papieren?

The
Nazis
aren't
coming
for
your
papers.

They
learned
written
words
can't
be
trusted.

So
if
you
think
they'll
ask
first
and
shoot
later,

you
probably
don't
belong
on
this
train.

We
are
going
to
the
Front.

# I Fall in Love

Dude.

I think I'm in love.

She watches sports.
She likes music.
She has animals.
She said something about traveling.

And did I mention
she has hobbies?
I don't know what they are
but damn, son.

Hobbies.

If she eats food,
she's the One.

## Lily and I

I said to Lily
as I walked to her pen, apple in hand,
*Lily, if only I were a horse,*
*you'd be my gal.*
And she neighed, looked at me for a long moment,
chewing.

...

Then she said
*Chigger, if only I were a man,*
*you'd be my gal.*

I still bring her apples
but we don't talk like we used to.

# Pee-Shivers

I
smoke
a
joint
and
drain
a
six
shooter
of
tall
boys.

Everytime
I
do
this
I
piss
all
ninety-six
ounces
in
one
standing,

wondering
if
I'll
ever
finish,

waiting
for
the
rain
to
stop,

convince
myself
it's
a
world
record,

when
pee-shivers
shake
me
to
the
core.

## Truisms Form a Yes-Set

(You are)           breathing,

                           you are conscious

(Aware)            of the book's binding

                           and feel the paper weight

                           as you read ink stains on

                           wood pulp.

*(paraphrasing Dale Carnegie)*

Remember who you are dealing with —

not creatures of logic
      but emotion

             bristling

                  with prejudice

           motivated by pride

and vanity.

# Muses are People,
# People are Animals

                                  She was constantly stealing
                                  my sentiment
on a whim.                     Give me words —
                                  I came for poetry.
I am not a person           here for the poetry,
                                  here watching my friends
                                        die on stage
                                  and come to life again
                                      in poetry.

I stay away from
the people and places
that remind me
    find love

(no comment).

See, muses                     (and people)
are animals.

## Road Smells

road smells of tarmac
petrol
damp of fresh rain
dry dust
sticky and sweet
road kill
rotting

a skunk
tells my inner child
a fart joke

I laugh in the face of Death

write it on the steering wheel
at 65 mph

and sneer
too old for that
but not too young to die

still

wouldn't mind
hitting a joint
that smelled half
so rank

# I Say It out Loud

        I am the blue knight    blue night blue ink
Ain't no one here heard of a vegetable

1     In a small Missouri town, in the winter 18
2     years after the turn of the Millenia (21st)
3     a man sat in a dingy cafe, sipping coffee
4     and reading a moldy translation of
5     The Book of Five Rings
6
7
8
9
10
11
12
13

Poetry makes it palatable
even the bodies — even the bodies
laugh x $\infty$ tears 4 evar

it doesn't make sense
that's jazz~ baby!
it's

                                    fireflies at night

## She Said, Pt.1

*Liber Novus* makes an appearance
on the diary of a militant feminist
doe eyed in the dark
sipping on single cups of coffee.

Remember when you broke your antenna and
we laughed about it for hours — the LuLz
that's how you make white people laugh
on a Precarious K-turn.

She said love is everything and
that's when it came for me
for the driver — this chupacabra
carrying a sword in it's teeth.

## She Said, Pt.2

Nail the weasel down
when the enemy is illiterate
buy out the folks who own civilization
open cell
free society

love is everything and
we still carry swords in our teeth.

## Two Things: First, I Foolishly Write a Great Deal of My Work While Driving on the Long Stretches of Interstate Highway Between Readings (Sorry Maha) and Second, This Poem Is Called *Crash*

When I was writing in your basement at 4 AM
alone in a house full of ghosts
hell dogs roamed the hallways and
mother dearest watched over every shoulder.
RATS-! I left my pad — all that fruit!
Echo — when we talk about him, he wins.

I am password I am code I am cypher.
I am hot to trot I am good to go.
I am skippin' town I am gettin' the heck outta Dodge.
I am on top of the world I am down and out.
I am on the prowl I am on the warpath.
I am on the way I am outta sight.
I am rockstar paperman scissorhand.
I am a fairly dangerous man.
I am not in Kansas anymore.

My body and my world
                      what I perceive to be intersect my soul

    from which I address you
humble servant to the Seat of All-Power:

| my God   | and my God's God |              |
|----------|------------------|--------------|
| my self  | my neighbor      | my enemy     |
| my seed  | my blood         | my teeth     |
| my child | my cousin        | my adversary |

to prevent poets from sliding into obscurity

time fears no thing but the pyramids

and so on and so on and so on
and the wheels are turning
and I can't stop writing
and I'm barreling down the highway
and I hope I don't!

## Gee Thanks, Maha

Matthew I'm so disappointed
this is not your best work
                         that was before
                         they crucified Spongebob

       my mother is
       a constellation

you got 10 toe-holds
you got two feet

                         moron globularia
                         (as idiots and tits)

(for Steve Vogt)


Some of these kids'd tear up
        a dream —
wilder'n peach orchard hogs
        these dire childrens.

*Hvarnuh!*


Errant Magus-
run interference
and be that roiling
chaos you hold
within; interlocutor
do you object to
resistance? Do you
quail before your
foes? NO! Happy
days when my
enemy stands before
me – now he will
be destroyed! That
is my gladness and
greatest joy!
*Hvarnuh!*\*

---

*\*Hvarnah has been an important tradition and symbol for Persians throughout their long history. A semantic development of the word was probably from a meaning of 'a desirable thing' to 'good fortune' and to khvarrah, written as a Semitic ideogram GDH in Middle Persian, with a particular meaning 'kingly glory or majesty.*

## This Is the Test

only open this letter if you are prepared —
because you seem happy I want very much
to please you —
this letter is true
what is true is not always pleasing
I would not like to upset you so I must warn you if
you should like to go on believing as you do —
do not open this letter

## Four Lords and a Lady

For some months of waiting
how apropos
that at our meeting again
nothing changes

no interruptions
                no touching
                              no interference
but it smells nice and the slave-girl
      is very beautiful:
              catches me in the pipe-dream
                and knows it
cause she ignores my table, professionally

what a pain — such a pose
writing for company
alone.

## Ero

I could write from the tips of your toes
to the nape of your neck
cover you in the ink of my ten hundred thousand words
you would be the body of my work
and I will have only just begun.

## Gasoline

ties my surrogate brotherhood together
and I often wonder what kind of fears
do grown men keep?
Even before the heathen came
it wasn't always sunshine and butterflies.

## *Mani Padme Hum Shiva*

I had a singing bowl
don't remember how I got it
only there it was
as suddenly in my hands
as if it had been there my whole life
its proportions perfect purr
under the wooden cudgel stirring
brass Sanskrit echoes into infinity
I held the pitch and whine
of an air-raid siren broadcasting
tranquility like an atom bomb
to the universal tune of $\Omega$

## I Know My Rights

There is one right — only one —
only one right anyone can infringe upon
which challenges the immediate exercise
of the one self-same right:
live or die.

All other mystic 'rights'
merely convenient lies
masturbatory, self-congratulations
only one right — only one —

all else is idyll
the fever-dream of a deathly civilization
taken to mind camps
to meditate with dogs.

## Introspect

doesn't take a pair of binoculars
to see my desk
two empty coffee cups and a lite beer later
I'll write about God or some chick
        or whatever

thinking: man
        cannot live by bread alone

but it sure beats digging through your garbage heart
for the restaurant leftovers you never eat

## She-Wasps

Adjusted
to
the
format

as
I
watched
a
heron
fly

Aphrodite
sat
at
my
shoulder
reclining,

scratching
expectantly

ticks
and
spiders

make
girls
take
off
their
clothes.

What
is
beyond
pleasant?

Not
much
of
a
swimmer

but
she
can
lizard-out.

Apparently
these
are
the
kinds

of
things
girls
say,

*The*
*growlers*
*are*
*better*
*fresh*
*and*
*they're*
*still*
*looking*
*for*
*servers.*

Imagine
that:
an
empire
wants
slaves.

Inwardly
I
said
*freedom*
*forever!*

While
three
witches
chanted

*We*
*don't*
*have*
*to*
*react*
*to*
*the*
*stick,*

like
they
were
bitches

slobbering
over
dick.

# Firefly Royalty in Garden Regalia at Purple Dusk

Do
me-!
Do
me-!
Signal
lightning
bugs
thundering
across
the
Ozark
and
God
willing
they'll
all
get
laid
tonight
it's
really
something
to
see

all
those
little
flashing
lights
while
angels
herd
cloud
cattle
rolling
in
the
wane.

## Ozark Knights

Ozark
knights
are
drinking
beer
on
a
back
porch
playing
hooky
from
their
wives
while
coon-dogs
lounge
between
patio
furniture.

I'm
listening
to
two

old
men
recall
horseback
riders
Osage
and
Irish,
what
were
then
cowboys
and
Indians.

When
these
old
soldiers
turned
to
me
and
asked
if
I
would
join

their
cause
I
had
to
wonder:
Elder,
why
do
you
seek
my
council?
But
what
I
said
was,
Yes.
We
will
take
Jerusalem.

(for Anna Pietrzak)

I have always admired the enduring nature of architects.
I daydream of building new pyramids: I daydream I'm
Pharaoh-reborn.

Words have a kind of lasting effect, like stone
or steel structures, but flighty.
I have crafted you a poem
and I have labored
                pain   stak   ing   ly
                           ov    er
                           ev    er   y
                                  syl  la  ble.

You see, that is my strength,
       whereas you—
you have a good eye,
                a steady hand,

                              and strong taste.

The gifts you made use of — your talents — will last.
And mine?
                Mine are already being carried away

                              on the turn of another page.

## Working on My Car

Somewhere I think to myself
it is Wednesday
and what's more humbling than that?
A razor the size of a rabbit's tooth
falcon feet.
Fact is you're not here
and hay bales golden buck teeth
> of ol' time romancers are distant memories
> of faded glory.

This is to say nothing about the Department of Transportation,
> the Army Corps of Engineers, or
> local law enforcement

in the summer.
Flowers bloom where they are.
I think this is beautiful while I change a flat tire:
how art is idle,
a kind of heavy air
about as useful as a cold beer
> to an already drunk baby and how

it is Wednesday.

## Optimism and Confidence

On the road this poetry conquers and consumes
rawhide
razorback
city-slickin'
riverbilly
northward ho-!
On the static banks of the Gasconade River
red quinoa crawls with ants
somehow semiotically related to
masturbation which is interesting in
light of Lincoln's famous words,
*I would rather watch a man fight bees*
and I have to agree,
it beats watching a man defend himself from
ants in his pants.

## Memory

No birdsong is as beautiful as your human voice
and truth is, I wish you'd shut the fuck up.
Echos and mirrors over a
vaulted ceiling channel two
abysses staring into electric introspective
jack-in-a-box
       with a fox
              wearing socks
recalling childhood ambitions
horizons and steel-beams or else
       green canopies will turn
              brown in the Fall
                      become gray and
                              die while yet living.
I see now that
this is another poem
about a road.

# And Anyway
*(for Jason Ryberg)*


You know what they say about
horses and water and
sticks and stones and
life and lemons.

You know what they say about
apples and trees and
chips and blocks.

You know what they say
about early birds and
chasing two rabbits and
blind squirrels.

You know what they say about
building Rome and
mountains and molehills and
the journey of a thousand miles.

You know what they say about
Greeks and gifts and
lookin' horses in the mouth and
birds and hands and bushes and
dogs and days.

You know what they say about
cooks and kitchens and
stopped clocks and
stones and moss.

You know what they say about
geese and ganders and
fish and water and
birds of a feather.

You know what they say about
forests and trees and
apples and oranges and
apples and apples.

And anyway,

what's that got to do with the price of tea in China?

## Sleep Walking

*Todays a new day,* I said.

hitting the snooze button,

*yes, today's the day I really make
something of myself,*
said I,

dozing off;

I wanted to do some pushups,

strangely found myself walking to the refrigerator
gnawing on leftover fried chicken and
a handful of strawberries,
drinking beer until I woke up
at noon.

## A Mind Camp Intern Meditates with Dogs

Every day
for fourteen days
an armadillo woke up dead.
For two weeks
the porchwood drank bloodstains in layers.
We threw the bodies in the river
unashamed of our pride, of our
remorseless
amoral
killers.

But the dogs are good
ol' boys and girls.

## Four Seasons Poem

Dead wood

Green shoots

Blood noon

Fresh meat

## Affluenza

Learning is a kind of ignorance
the same way
remembering is forgetting
in the decadence of loftiest spaces
at the flatitudes on top of the world
there

in pillow prisons
people are captives
of comfort.

## *Momento Mori* (from *The Travelers Guide to Psychometry*)

grim disposition that
washes dust with a metal brush
grim the boy, the man, the forgetful
mother of sorrows
and our suffering
if it were coked up on highway blood
eased by waiting, watchful Death

noble buzzards

rescue me from undying shame
solid as rocks and rigor mortise,
gorge on my innards and
rub some dirt on me so
I can claim internment
buried beside the road
silent as the grave
then I can join the grateful dead

future people will remember my
white cross and wreath

*here lies X-Y-Z*
*didn't wear a helmet*

*or died drunk*
*or was a child*
*or whose bladder exploded*

casualties of road wars
line yellow stripes in bleach bone,
tufts of mangy hair, the occasional
tooth, and
abandoned teddy bears

# Moonshot (from *The Travelers Guide to Psychometry*)

*yaa we'll shoot for the moon—*
*getting there*
*is another thing altogether*

take into account
how much money you
don't feel bad asking for,
add that to the list
of apples oranges and
bananas at 1.47$ a pound

like Pop and Maha used to say
*in my day,*
*gallon was a quarter*
but in future times bananas
are extinct and gas is
more precious than amber wave

radios signal interdimensional
rollercoaster head or
how we know when to
make ginger and cinnamon tea to
cure the ups and downs of
longitudinal malaise and time
travel by tarot

another word for rota
by wheel in the skyward direction
bobble-head swivel and
turn to see Wichita and Sioux
fall defenders on Calvary
with horses too, but in America
and armed with lightning from
maw Golgotha charnel

so now they stand sentinel as
Ghost of Black Cloud
avenged by every whipping
cyclone that beat
those humble-bloodstained
mobile homes to death
(to death! To death!) granting
visions of buffalo riots
flaming stag of prairie fire
and the moon looks on

intersex
juxtaposed
indifferent

# Window Roller (from *The Travelers Guide to Psychometry*)

rolling down windows
to clear the air

dense thoughts are
glad to feel a breeze

there is no music on
the horizon is roaring past

a woman commands the wind
and the wind is a man that moves her

the history of clouds signals
smoke curling at the window

dark skies prompt
prayers from everyone

*Lord*
but that's all he prays

*Christ*
but that's all she prays

*Hell*
but that's all I pray

fingering the sill
between two worlds

how small is a poem
compared to a road?

or a psychometrists unwieldy touch
to the history of time?

Plains Indians
ride and

I am about to sink
deep in it again when

rain smacks my weather
veined hand
and I roll up the windows

## Dirge of Lightning Bugs (from *The Travelers Guide to Psychometry*)

more than one—

four
are corners of your blessing
by winds gale and zephyr
tightly in arms that hold your trust; and
rampant is your gospel

your carpet is cross-stitched with
magic and soaring
now you are riding high
while

on Earth I make your mark:
by the flowing waters above and
below I drink to your good glory;
tearful libations an ode to joy

this triune sign is fire
for all great bellies hold fire:
sun above, son of man, and
lowly lightning bug

in reverie I swear I am
from somewhere else;

note, coincidentally,
we are making good time and

turn on wipers
streaking what I imagine are
thunderous peals of
bioluminescence

# LIGHTNING VAJRA! (from *The Travelers Guide to Psychometry*)

at 0400 creepy
jammin' out
a monster in motion
barreling down highway...

whatever

I don't remember which one
and I had a notion

wouldn't it be great to be a successful businessman?
how very Japanese, blinking hard against the stars
non-sequitur cartoons giggled up
and I had a notion

my ride is forged from the mystic particulate
of Saturn's rings
it protects from dark magic
even if it is a bit dusty
when suddenly-
(remember I am traveling at dangerous speeds)

      LIGHTNING VAJRA!

I am going sideways
fish tailing on dew drops worth of water
then belly up
and hanging out

I think I must have fallen
asleep

send help

## The Universal Sign for Choking or *Ek-! Ek-!*

There's a whole clove of garlic
lodged in my throat.

I ate the whole clove 'cause I felt sick;
        garlic is supposed to fix that.

I'm dying and
        trying to remain calm.

At thirty seconds, I think
        this is so stupid, then write,

*Fill up on feelings*
*Keep eating*

*Choke on them*
*Die.*

It's been a good minute since my last breath;
I almost black out but

the last line makes me laugh and
I hack up the garlic clove.

It's covered in that stringy throat porno saliva so
I utter *Glory Be* before

I swallow it whole and
try again.

Chigger Matthews is a language artist living in the American Midwest. Hosts the collaborative feature *Free Chigger Matthews Presents*, teaches poetry workshops for all ages, and is an artist-in-residence at Osage Arts Community in Belle, MO. He is the chief editor for *The Artifact, Planet Earth's First Global Poetry Newspaper* and his work appears at home and abroad.

This project was made possible, in part, by generous support from the Osage Arts Community.

Osage Arts Community provides temporary time, space and support for the creation of new artistic works in a retreat format, serving creative people of all kinds — visual artists, composers, poets, fiction and nonfiction writers. Located on a 152-acre farm in an isolated rural mountainside setting in Central Missouri and bordered by ¾ of a mile of the Gasconade River, OAC provides residencies to those working alone, as well as welcoming collaborative teams, offering living space and workspace in a country environment to emerging and mid-career artists. For more information, visit us at www.osageac.org

Osage Arts Community

www.ingramcontent.com/pod-product-compliance
Lightning Source LLC
Chambersburg PA
CBHW021450080526
44588CB00009B/784